MW00770089

Coaching Basketball:
Unboxed Wisdom

By

Dr. Bill Ciancio

Copyright 2019
Sunset Angel Productions, LLC

Lahaina, Hawaii 96761
(808) 345-5411 phone
www.sapllc.us

Published by ebookit.com

ISBN-13: 978-1-4566-334-86

Contents

Disclaimer

My coaching career started in the early 1960s.
My basketball vocabulary and many references
date my experiences back to those days. You
younger readers may not relate to this
terminology. However, you will be a more well-
rounded coach after researching many of my
references. You must be patience with my
vocabulary. I can best describe my experiences in
the terms of the times they happened. After
accepting this disclaimer, off you go into
exploring my world of coaching basketball.

Acknowledgements

The support from my wife and kids was unconditional. They encouraged me to write this book about my extensive coaching experiences. My current assistant coach, Lalo, happens to be an English teacher and helped edit parts of this manuscript. Thanks Lalo for your help and suggestions.

Introduction

The title <u>Coaching Basketball: Unboxed Wisdom</u> became obvious when I began editing this book. Wisdom is the combination of knowledge and experiences tempered with good judgment. My basketball knowledge encompasses the history of the game. My coaching experiences span over five decades. Time has peppered my judgment with insights beyond winning and losing games. Visualizing your impact on players, officials, parents, administrators and fans points to the wisdom I am addressing.

My thoughts of becoming a serious basketball coach began after watching the Konawaena High School Boy's basketball team play in the fall of 1974. My first impression was that I could do a better job coaching. Not until many years later did I realize that coaching basketball or any sport can be hazardous to one's ego! Like figuring out how to be a successful coach isn't as easy as saying "I can do a better job!" I have gained a tremendous amount of respect for the game and the coaches trying to coach it. My ideas of how basketball SHOULD be coached are just another way of 'peeling the preverbal banana!'

While many of the principles discussed in this book may be applied to other team sports, basketball is this book's focus. Several overlapping sports concepts may be used to emphasize a point as it applies to coaching the game of basketball. I will also use the pronouns he or him to indicate the players. This is no slight on girls and women's sports. Appropriate team coaching techniques apply no matter the gender.

My qualifications for writing this book come from coaching experiences spanning almost 60 years, beginning in 1959 through the present (2019). My knowledge of the game comes from reading over 100 basketball 'How to' books and attending many coaching clinics. Also, child-rearing books proved to be an important relationship source for working with my players. My professional, non-coaching career, also adds to my perspective as I was not dependent on a coaching career for my livelihood.

As captain of my grade-school, intramural teams, a parish priest noticed my enthusiasm for basketball. He encouraged my enthusiasm through my graduation. When I was in high school he asked me to help him coach my younger brother's grade-school team. Together we coached the St. Celestine's team to 4th out of 300 teams in Chicago's Christian Youth League (CYO). I was hooked from then on and continued coaching CYO and grade school teams while attending college.

My formal coaching career began in institutions of higher learning. I quickly realized that my youthful approach to friendships and business concepts did not apply to educational institutions. My wrong assumptions became personal and soured my respect for many priorities within education. I assumed that everyone in education wants to explore, streamline and improve ways of doing things. That simple assumption got me fired from my coaching duties several times. In those cases, my mistake was not bowing to mediocrity.

I have always been blessed with an adventurous spirit. I moved from one coaching position to another with a sense of renewal. Along the way my coaching philosophy has evolved, de-evolved and evolved again to its present form.

This book celebrates the evolution of my judgment calls while combining basketball knowledge and experience. <u>Coaching Basketball: Unboxed Wisdom</u> highlights this journey.

"Everyone thinks of changing the world, but no one thinks of changing himself." – Leo Tolstoy

Chapter 1 Foundation

Think of a building's foundation. It's solid, well-formed and lasts for long periods of time. Building your coaching philosophy should be the same. It should be formed on basic, stable principles. One of many principles I used early on in my coaching career was, 'Treat others the way I wanted to be treated.' My 'Treat' principle formed the cornerstone to my player and team management ideas. Find principles that you live by and apply these to coaching.

The things that you learn about coaching basketball carry over into coaching other team sports. Developing player-coach relationships is the same no matter what the sport.

Chances are you may coach more than one sport. Basketball drew me into coaching, but I have coached soccer, softball, football and baseball. I use the same player and team management approach for coaching all sports. The only thing that changes is the X's and O's. What I'm telling you is that the basic way your approach your players, practices and parents should be similar in every sport you coach. Keep that in mind as you form the foundations of your basketball coaching philosophy.

Your coaching foundation helps to build and understand your system. That is the only way you can confidently teach your system to players. This foundation includes a philosophy of play and how you approach various team elements. Whenever you are coaching children through teenagers, you'll have parents and administrators watching. If they don't like what they're seeing, you may be out of a coaching position quicker then you'd like.

Every coach has a personality they cannot shed. The best advice I can give you is to maintain an even temperament. When you do have to raise your voice, do it in a non-demeaning manner. Never attack a player's personhood or background. Treat ALL players the same on the practice floor or field. Off the court that's a different story. However, becoming friends with players can have negative results depending on the circumstances. My advice to you is to stay gossip free. Coaches today have to pretend that they live in a glass house. Like your actions in public are ALWAYS open to interpretation.

With that part of your foundation addressed we can continue focusing on basketball. In the 1970s I started coaching higher level basketball. That's when I became a serious reader. I would visit book stores in every city I visited. When I grew tired of reading contemporary basketball books, I began finding older basketball books in antique stores. I purchased books authored by older basketball coaches such as Claire Bee, Adolph Rupp and James Naismith (the creator of the game).

I immediately recognized that basketball books concentrated on plays. The X's and O's of how to score and/or play defense. They would advocate for a specific system that worked for them and their teams. They could show you on a chalkboard (dry erase, these days) how the play was executed to get easy, open shots. Or they could show you how their defense stops all sorts of scoring. Of course, no offense or defense scheme is perfect!

I went to coaching clinics and listened to coaches' compare plays and argue how their plays were better. Then I can to a realization one night as several of us coaches sat around relaxing. The coach with the chalk last would win the discussion.

All young coaches try running plays because that's what their mentors teach. That was how old-style basketball was taught. Winning coaches would use a high-post offense and others would try to copy it. Or a collegiate champion would use a 2-3 zone, and soon the 2-3 zones became the defensive standard. Young coaches didn't analyze the players playing these systems.

Let's look at the collegiate game. College coaches recruit players. Not only do they recruit the best players, but they recruit the best players for their specific system. An excellent example is Jim Boeheim at Syracuse. His defense of choice is the 2-3 zone. Look at the players he recruits to play that zone. They are tall, quick and lankly with longer than average wingspans. His offense needs players that can create their own shots. He's been so successful that he's been coaching at Syracuse University for over 40 years.

If you're coaching a team with similar player characteristics, you may have the same sort of success as Coach Boeheim. Chances are your players are a mixture body types with a variety of skills. So, if you decide to play a 2-3 zone, you may want to modify Coach Boeheim's zone slides to incorporate the kinds of players available to you.

After the 'Wooden Years' (UCLA's National Championship runs between 1961-1975) coaches began to say, 'to win you need the best players.' And true to that idea, many high school and collegiate coaches would cheat to get those best players. At the collegiate level in addition to academic scholarships - money, cars, parent gifts, etc would change hands. At the high school level, schools began recruiting and bribing players, similar to that at the collegiate level. Either through their boosters or the school itself coaches bought players they through would win championships for them.

This is where we are today. Even the most ethical collegiate coaches are opting to recruit the 'one and done' future NBA player. The 'one and done' term applies to a player that plays college ball for only one year and is then drafted into the professional ranks for large sums of money. With the right combination of peer pressure and team culture, those coaches are the majority of participants during the National Collegiate Athletic Association's (NCAA) annual Final Four Tournament today!

Your coaching philosophy will encompass a variety of morals, ethics and emotions. We all want to win. Ask yourself, 'What is the cost of winning?' A scandal-free career has always been my goal. Sleeping comfortably is my guide to how I'm doing. My conscious resting peacefully is more important than winning. What's your ethics guide going to be?

Your emotions are very unstable and should never be the foundation for direction in your life. – Joyce Meyer

Chapter 2 Why

So you want to become a basketball coach. WHY? What are you getting out of coaching players to win? And what does winning mean to you?

What motivates coaches to coach can be summarized in the broadest of terms. I believe basketball coaches have four main motivators. Any one of these motivators makes coaching very addictive.

Ask yourself this multiple choice question. Is your desire to coach basketball totally ego-centered, competition motivated, encouragement-driven or all the above? These are all good reasons in the coach's mind. But all three individually lead us down different paths. Each path by itself has pitfalls and can lead to disastrous results. Most mature coaches have a bit of each woven into their fabric or number four - all the above.

Today, the totally ego-driven coach will probably do anything to get the best players. These 'rule breakers' are generally angry coaches. The ego-driven coach ultimately salvages his integrity by gathering a perspective of life in the real world. I use the word gathering because we all have to live a variety of life's experience to mature and appreciate its big picture. Within the big picture, many coaches ultimately realize the wisdom of a balanced perspective. Our spiritual, mental, emotional and physical well-being keeps many egos in check.

The competition-driven personality will most likely abuse his players. Sometimes that's why you see players transfer from one school to another. This Machiavellian approach to coaching keeps the competitive-driven coach on edge blaming players for the team's failures. As with the ego driven coach, a balanced, thankful attitude can keep the coaches' competitive nature relatively in check.

The encouragement-driven personality has a tough time in today's society. Boosters, administrators and fans want wins. If a coach doesn't win, he'd better have a friendly, decision-making administrator watching his back! The encouragement coach, overlooks negatives, finds positives and tries to keep his player's well-being in mind. He is a player's buddy sometimes.

Parents get caught in the same frame-of-mind. Just like parenting, the principle of accountability needs to begin to apply in varying degrees as children mature. The key to a mature player/coach relationship is respect. Respect can only come from when players and coaches hold each other accountable. Should any friendship develop between player and coach, it grows out of respect for each other.

A variety of combinations may evolve from the three possibilities above. Coaches need a certain amounts of ego to show their players his confidence in teaching the game plan. A coach needs to show his or her competitive nature. If the players sense the coach doesn't care about winning, why should they!

Every coach must encourage players. John Wooden used the 'praise, scold, praise' method of encouragement. The praise gets the player's attention. The scold corrects the incorrect play. The praise concludes with 'you're okay' type of message. The bottom line is, coaches must build up a player's confidence. Only confident players win the big games.

Later in my coaching career, I learned a simple phrase that keeps me in the 'all the above' category. "Players don't care much you know. They care about how much you care!" Balance is a huge key to living a contented life. Balance is the key to why coaches are successful. Quality coaches build relationships and respect from players and friends alike!

Let's sum up "Why are you coaching?" It is for yourself or for others. Answering that question will give you direction and maybe some peace of mind. I look back on my coaching career and see players not wins. I hear their voices of thanks for leadership and encouragement. I am proud that they are successful, participating members of society!

"Developing better people should be the number one goal for any coach when dealing with kids" – Bobby Orr

Chapter 3 Now What

Early in my coaching career I began realizing I had to win with lesser talent then many of our opponents. I began playing the role of a serious, no non-sense coach. I believed it the saying, 'My way or the highway'. Only problem was, my way was laced with lots of enthusiasm but little substance.

Most schools with successful programs don't change coaches. Your first head coaching position will probably be with a team with a losing record. My earliest head coaching positions came with teams and losing records. I had to figure out a way to win. I went into my coaches' role. I didn't smile much and demanded perfection from my players. Only later in my coaching career did I realize that wasn't me! I was acting like I thought coaches should act.

I was competitive by nature, but not willing to break the rules. I was left with a dilemma. How can I win and still keep my integrity? Honestly, I didn't know basketball very well but I knew people. Unrealistically, I began picturing my players better than they actually were.

I challenged them to run fast breaks. The problem with playing fast-paced basketball are the turnovers. I eventually developed a set a drills that would lower the number of predictable turnovers. That was easy. We practiced running, passing and shooting with the ball on the run! From the early days of my coaching career, transition basketball has become my specialty.

I coached a team defense made famous by Bobby Knight, the 'Help and Recover' defense. The challenge is getting players to play defense with enthusiasm. I tried a variety of methods. Honestly, I don't like defense either. To make defense exciting for me and ultimately for my players, I had to connect it to the offense. I eventually combined 'Help and Recover' ideas with stealing passes from the weak side. I eventually replaced the term 'weak side or help side' with steal side.

While I was in the process of developing transition and defensive drills that fit my philosophy, my teams won with enthusiasm and sheer grit. I expected to win. Soon the players began to expect to win too. We didn't win league championships early on but we did win our share of upsets. We won enough games that I looked forward to every next season after that. That's when I realized I needed to assemble and formalize my philosophy, practice and game plans.

Soon I began to research the game itself. I learned a lot of basketball from books and I tried a variety of different plays. My enthusiasm for new ideas kept me and my players involved and playing hard.

Not until I stepped out of coaching for several years to tend to my young family did I really begin to understand the game. I began to study the college game in the 1970's. The Final Fours (March Madness) were still low key events. I attended every Final Four during the 1980's. I met such greats as Jim Valvano (North Carolina State), Ray Meyers (De Paul), Digger Phelps (Notre Dame), Marv Harshman (Washington) and Rollie Massimino (Villanova) to name a few.

These greats exemplified quite a variety of coaching personalities. My stereotype of how a coach should act went out the window. Basically, I lightened up and tried not to live and die on every win or loss. From there my coaching maturity began to evolve. But I will admit, I did hold the officials accountable in many a close game.

These greats also explained their philosophies about the game. Valvano was a defensive trickster. Harshman was a straight meat and potatoes fundamentals type. His classic quote was "little guys get tired, big guys don't shrink!" Massimino had the 'squeeze blood from a rock' player demeanor. Phelps loved his cigars and enjoyed life away from the court with Bobby Knight. They were all so different but they all had one thing in common. They were all winning games and having fun coaching.

I came to two conclusions after meeting these greats. I decided I needed to be myself. I could not act like Mr. Authority Coach and have fun coaching. Also, I learned that being competitive doesn't lend to having fun unless you have a philosophy about how to play the game. Since then, I have made fun a priority.

Once you begin to coach, you should develop a 'never stop learning' attitude. I realized that while going back into coaching for the third time in my career.

As I aged into my 60's, I had to earn some retirement money for my family. At the beginning of your career, you must realize that coaching basketball only monetarily rewards a few coaches at the university level. Those coaches make millions of dollars. The majority of us coaches wind up becoming public or private school teachers. Take it from me; teachers don't make enough money to be the only supporting income for a family without means.

During that time I was a coach on the outside looking in. I was fortunate to be on the Maui Invitational Tournament medical staff for several years. I watch dozens of Division I teams practice and play, up-close and personal.

During some of those secessions, I imagined how I would coach these huge, talented DI players. They all seemed to have the same abilities. Why did some play like winners and others play like losers? Then I noticed their coaches' demeanor and style.

The younger head coaches practiced drills without any connection to their offenses or sometimes even their defenses. The older coaches progressed though practice making connections with their game plans and philosophy. As a bonus, they were having fun.

This realization confirmed my coaching philosophy and how it was developed. I have the confidence that I could coach at any level because of my reasons for coaching and the foundations I have already put down.

"Nothing in the world is more common than unsuccessful people with talent." – Anonymous

Chapter 4 Philosophy

Every coach should try to develop his own coaching philosophy. That means you need an idea of how you want to play in ALL phases of the game, including how to run your practices and manage your public relations. My philosophy came naturally through experiences and temperament.

As a young player I realized I could out run anyone on the basketball court. So when my team would get the defensive rebound, I would race out in front of the pack. When my teammates passed me the ball, I would go in for an easy layup. I was good for 10 to 20 points a game starting in the fifth grade. In high school I would get five or six easy layups every game.

Today, we call what I did, 'cherry picking'. I naturally figured out by anticipating my team getting the defensive rebound, I could beat the opponents up court by sprinting up court before the other team could react. When my teammates saw me open, they would pass me the ball. Easy baskets are what most offenses long to get.

My temperament is another story. Once I realized that I was goal-oriented and impatient, my coaching philosophy began to develop more clearly. I found myself telling my teams to run and score quickly. Only problem was, my teams seemed out of control. Through the parenting ideas I referenced earlier in this book, I realized I needed to tell the players HOW TO run more efficiently. That's when I started scouting college teams that ran and scored successfully. I investigated the different parts of their systems.

Some college systems concentrated entirely on running and shooting within seven seconds of getting the ball. Their entire philosophy revolved around getting the ball. I tried that system one season as a head coach. I drove one of my assistant coaches absolutely crazy. He was defensive minded. That year we scored over 100 points in seven 32 minute games. We even lost one game 107 to 106!

As in life that game plan needed balance, much to the liking of my trusted assistant coach. I gave him the defense. Together we developed a defensive philosophy of disruption. I have further taken that idea and figured out many ways of disrupting opponents offensives.

Most coaches go through a similar progression. They copy a winning system with some success. Understanding the philosophy behind that system is the key to incorporating parts of it into your own philosophy. Then you have a better understanding of how to teach and modify the system to your liking.

I encourage young coaches to pick up different elements from different systems. As you're doing that try to understand the philosophy behind each of those systems. Until you do those things, you will only have moderate success as I did. Not until I settled on a philosophy, did I mold it into a semi-permanent system. I use the word, 'semi' because I am always willing to update or modify as necessary.

Part of my winning theory is developing an 'edge'. What's your edge? Every coach needs an edge to win. Gathering talent and letting them play is the simplest, easiest and surest shortcut to winning. However, talent does not guarantee winning at the playoff levels, unless you have NBA - high school draftees on your team.

Getting the best players philosophy is basic playground basketball. Those of us who are familiar with winning on the local blacktop know one thing. Get the best players on your team and let them carry the team's scoring. The rest of us play some defense and we'll hold the court until we're exhausted.

Average talent can win with more than its share with an 'edge'. Sometimes they can win deep into playoffs, if they believe they have an edge on the other teams. That's the coaches' job. If you are not a just 'throw out the balls' type of coach, you want to win with style. To win you need an edge with average talent. In your philosophy there is a winning edge. By becoming an expert in one specific phase of the game, your team will automatically develop that edge.

One example would be an edge in conditioning. When you develop full-court drills and scrimmages for your practices your team will have an edge in conditioning. Through your practice procedures and overall philosophy, your team can play more efficiently for longer periods in the game. Players will believe you have this conditioning edge when you tell them, if for no other reason than the sweat on their practice jerseys at the end of practice!

Your philosophy extends to choosing your players. What type of player do you want to coach? Choosing your players can make or break an average talented team. Even a very talented team without discipline can be a nightmare and sometimes causes coaches to be fired.

Do you want compliant, 'Happy Days' type players or do you want the inmates from the local jailhouse types? Whatever types of players you want on your team, you must have rules. Since the word 'rules' has judgmental undertones in society today, I have changed that part of my philosophy to 'standards'.

The standards I use are Play Hard, Play Together and Have Fun. During preseason I will loosely elaborate on what those terms mean to our team. For example, Having Fun means winning to me. I have fun winning. I know all competitive players like winning. So it's not too hard to get players' buy-in and begin to create a winning team culture. I emphasize winning with poise and class!

I can't give you a philological check list. You may dissect your philosophy into as many parts as you what. I apply the acumen 'KISS' – Keep It Simple Stupid as a theme for my philosophy. Overall I tell my players that practices are mine. The games are yours. Always indicating they are to play WHAT we practice in our practices!

Ultimately, I have an offensive, defensive, transition, practice and game philosophies. I will elaborate how I chose these in the next chapter.

Coaches should always try to improve on their coaching skills. That concept applies to my players, too. I believe every player and team should be trying to get better every practice, every game. With that mentality, I can logically push for perfection, knowing in the back of my mind that we will never be perfect. But that does not stop us from trying!

For some reason, I never cared much about winning league as much as I wanted to run deep into whatever level playoff system I was coaching. One of my main goals was to get better for every game. Post-season playoffs were our teams' reward for how close we came to accomplishing this goal.

I realize now that once we were in playoffs, our season is nearly over. For many years, my teams were as close to me as family. I didn't want our fun to end. But just like in parenting, we have to let our kids go to make their way in life. I survive the end of seasons by looking forward to the next season.

"I'm still waiting for perfection. In the meantime, I'll settle for persistence" – Bo Ryan

Chapter 5 Explore

When I began to get serious about coaching basketball, I looked for examples of great coaches. I found many super coaches. My problem I was looking for their perfect system. Not until I realized there is no perfect system that fit all my ideas did I start exploring specifics of each coaches system. Eventually, I came up with a patchwork quilt approach and built a system that fit my developing philosophy.

Unfortunately, today's young coaches don't have the types of mentors I had in the second half of the 1900s. Most coaches today at the Amateur Athletic Union (AAU), high school and collegiate levels use the 'find the best players' philosophy.

The 1972 Title IX federal legislation – women's sports equity – had a major effect on men's sports. At the high school and collegiate levels, the burden of funding women's sports team fell on men's teams. Large universities ramped up their football and men's basketball programs. These sports funded women's sports until they could support themselves. Many still have not become self-supporting.

With Title IX, men's basketball became more like professional basketball in the entertainment sense. Athletic directors needing to make money fostered the current coaching 'musical chairs' system within the major universities. Winning to fill arenas and stadiums with paying customers is today's norm.

Within the 'best' philosophy, not much coaching is happening at the major collegiate levels. But if you look hard there are a few coaches actually running game plans worth noting. North Carolina's Roy Williams' offensive transition has some structure. Tony Bennett of Virginia operates the highly copied 'Pac Line' defense. In my day, the 'Pac Line' was called a sagging men-to-man defense. Bill Self of Kansas runs a structured early offensive scheme. Michigan State's Tom Izzo, one of my favorites, runs many proven two and three man half-court plays.

All major collegiate basketball coaches have two things in common. They make millions of dollars and they fill arenas across the country. They and their respective football teams support ALL the non-revenue sports teams on campus, included women's sports teams mandated by Title IX legislation.

Coaches at the lower collegiate and high school levels have less talented players therefore requiring them to do more coaching. Tapping into their philosophy can be difficult but not impossible. In this modern age many coaches have made 'how to' videos covering all the many facets of coaching basketball's offense and defense. You have to familiarize yourself with a variety of offensives and defenses then search the Internet for the mentors you fancy who run them.

My exploration began with the coaches styles I admired. Below are some of my mentors and the ideas I took from them.

Offensively, I was attracted to Paul Westhead's system. I sat with him at a coaches' clinic I worked in Palm Springs, California. He explained his system and the amounts of daily practice time he spent working on it. I was amazed that his players ran his fast tempo system for a minimum of one and one-half hours EVERY practice. From Paul Westhead I learned the value of repetition, full court drills and conditioning.

From Dean Smith I appreciated the value of half-court offense and working the clock at the end of close games. Because of his 'Four Corners' offense with Phil Ford in the middle, the National Collegiate Athletic Association (NCAA) introduced a shot clock similar to that used in the professional National Basketball Association (NBA). Coach Smith fostered the concept of team 'family' that is so popular today. I have always tried to emulate Dean Smith's classy coaching demeanor and some of his half-court offenses.

From Jim Valvano's coaching stint at North Carolina State, I valued his improvising on the fly. I was privileged to sit next to him at a Final Four, Kodak dinner in the early 80s. I was attracted to his free-flowing personality. Fun was his middle name!

Valvano used an unconventional defensive style that confused many coaches in his day. His players may not have been as talented other

Atlantic Coast Conference (ACC) teams, but he would disrupt their highly vaulted half court offenses of the day with his improvised man defenses.

I still utilize some of his ideas in many games today. Most coaches today have not figured how to attack his defenses. That's because they do not understand the basic ideas behind these defenses and have no historical perspective.

Al McGuire was a character. He would ride his motorcycle to practices wearing jeans and a t-shirt. Sometimes he'd show up, stay for a half hour and leave. His personal life-style probably led to the three things I gleamed from him. He would recruit one superstar player, probably because Marquette wasn't any basketball powerhouse before he coached there. His superstar was his 'go to' guy in crutch time. His 'sting' philosophy used traps two or three times a game to get a few steals. The value of his 'sting defense' was to convert enough turnovers for the winning margin. Coach McGuire taught me to be my own man, have a 'go to' player and the value of trapping a few times a game.

My coaching style never favored Bob Knight. But to his credit, he got 'Machiavellian' results. I learned two things from him. My first defensive book was his soft cover 'Help and Recover Defense'. I'll always remember that cover. The cover had a devilish looking player in a defensive stance with long, pointy fingernails and smoke coming out of his nose. From that book not only did I learn his help and recover defense, but that the offensive man ALWAYS has an advantage. All of today's major defensive schemes use some form of Bob Knight's defense. I mostly learned that I did not want to emulate Coach Knight's aggressive, on court style of disciplining players. Eventually, his aggressiveness got him fired from Indiana University.

John Wooden taught me it's ok for a coach to be a scholar. He was an English teacher in the Midwest before moving to UCLA to coach their men's basketball team. He also taught English at UCLA. He spoke eloquently and I admired that. He didn't talk like a stupid jock coach. I did have a doctorate degree at the time I became a serious coach. I was fortunate to meet Coach Wooden twice at coaching clinics where I was on staff. I remember he was very old and needed help going up the platform stairs. He would sit on his stool and lecture us on his 'Pyramid of Success'.

Coach Wooden taught me several things. Early in my coaching career, I used his 2-2-1 zone press. I had marginal success. Not until many years later did I realize HOW he used the press so successfully. I learned that understanding the idea behind the defense or offense is more important than the X's and O's.

The most important practice idea I took from Coach Wooden was his ratio of 1 to 10. He claimed that basketball was a game of habits (similar to what Paul Westhead and others say) and these habits had to be repeated – daily. The way he did that was to keep his instruction time to one minute for every ten minutes of practice. I have modified that ratio during preseason. But once the season begins and the players know your practice drills, I would try to adhere to the 1 – 10 ratio.

Your challenge is to merge past proven basketball plays with the modern freestyle player. My advice is to find systems and coaches with which you can identify. Read and watch whatever your choice of basketball media. I like books. I have also found digital media can be extremely informative. Attend basketball clinics that feature your favorite coaches. Ask them clarifying questions until you understand 'how to' apply their ideas. Learn and use what you see. Filter their ideas with the way you want to play the game.

Finally, all the coaches you look to for ideas don't have to be basketball coaches. Author Dorothy Briggs isn't a basketball coach. She coaches parenting. Coaching is something like parenting providing care and nurturing for your players. The football coach, Lou Holtz, added much needed humor to my coaching style. Being a serious, goal oriented first born, I needed to lighten up my attitude from day one of my professional coaching career. My dad helped too. He had a sign nailed over his work bench in our garage. It read, 'Don't take life to seriously. You don't get out of it alive, anyways!'

Summing up, explore offenses and defenses that fit your developing philosophy.

Experiment with modifications to these existing offenses and defenses. Balance your approach to teaching them between serious and fun! Time and patience are the keys to seeing your creations work on the court.

"A successful man is one who can lay a firm foundation with the bricks others have thrown at him." – David Brinkley

Chapter 6 Choosing

A few mentor coaches may have helped form some of your coaching ideas. Eventually every coach has to come up with their own foundational beliefs and system. Now it's time to formalize and organize your ideas. You should classify your system's ideas into offense, transition, defense, practice and game. Program management and public relations are important and will be covered in the later chapters.

Modern offenses have equated the 3-pointer as the talent equalizer. Before the 3-point line, the tall teams had huge advantages. Like Marv Harshman, University of Washington, said, "Tall players don't shrink". Consequently, half-court offenses are using the 3-pointer to negate taller teams. Some of today's coaches use the 3-pointer in their early offense to overwhelm teams.

The modern basketball player loves making 3-pointers. I think they feel like they've hit a home run in baseball. For some less talented players, making a 3-pointer is like a gift from heaven. Point being, for some players, you should incorporate the 3-pointer in your offensive scheme.

Who and where you emphasize shooting the 3-pointer becomes obvious with your talent. I have experienced teaching shooting mechanics and 3-point spot shooting to an incoming high school player during summer workouts while coaching in Hawaii. I knew that our offensive scheme gave open 3-pointers in certain areas of our transition and half-court offense.

Marvin had the desire and determination to play even though he was barely 5 feet tall. He practiced for hours at our local playground. He would shoot from the top of the key for hours. He used his little brother to fetch rebounds for him. Marvin started for me his freshmen year and contributed two or three 3-pointers every game.

Marvin's story did not end there. He confided in me about his feelings of inferiority at being too short to play basketball, the game he loved. Fortunately, I learned to have empathy with my players from author Dorothy Briggs child rearing book, <u>Your Child's Self-Esteem</u>. My comment may have stuck with him because he went on to play four years of Division III basketball and graduate with a college degree in business.

Marvin's determination made him into man. My comment, "use your height to your advantage" motivated him to become a defensive wizard. He led our freshman team in steals while he was nailing 3-pointers at the other end of the court.

The above example is one of the many proud moments in this coaches' career. I would not have had the insight into how to coach Marvin if I did not develop a confident coaching foundation. Marvin also exemplifies that a young player's determination can move mountains.

Think about a player's determination when you choose players for your next team!

When choosing your defensive schemes, you have to account for the 3-point shot. Luckily, there are two sayings that give coaches confidence defending the 3-point shot. One saying, "live by the 3, die by the 3," means coaches that base their entire offense on the 3-point shot are like 'riverboat gamblers'! In other words they will win some but probably lose more. The other saying is, "defense wins championships." Most experienced coaches know that a combination of offense, defense and well coached players makes for great teams.

Your defense must fit your talent. With quick players, you can play several kinds of man-to-man defense. Remember, the offensive player always has a half second advantage knowing when to start an offensive move. Either a dribble, pass or shot, the offense always has the head start.

As a defensive coach you have to decide if your players are going to simply react to the offense or do something else. My personality does not like to be told what to do. I do not like another team dictating to my players where to move on the court. Therefore, I favor a disruptive type of defense. My team's defense is going to tell the offenses how and where they can move. And more importantly, my teams will dictate how fast they play the game.

My defensive evolution took time to develop. This book is a 'how to', not a 'what to do' coaching aid! Needless to say, you can choose from a variety of man-to-man and zone defenses. The fundamentals of both are the same. Players need to close-out, box-out, communicate and they need to help each other. The only differences are the responsibilities.

Most coaches only pay 'lip service' to the transition part of the game. There is an offensive to defensive transition. This is where coaches will use some sort of a press triggered by whatever they want to trigger it. An example might be that they press after made baskets. Or they'll press after made freethrows. Some coaches favor pressing throughout the entire game. If that's your style, you'd better have a deep bench or your players have to be in exceptional physical condition.

I favor the defense to offense transition. You know why from one of my earlier chapters. While you decide, you should know that many championship caliber teams play pressure defense, full and half-court. So, your team has to be prepared to face pressure defenses and still win.

When you consider the transition game, you are deciding whether or not to play the game on the entire court. If your players are quick and fast, you will have an advantage over slower teams. Coaches should understand that playing a full-court game requires more practice time dedicated to conditioning and confidence in your bench players.

You have many ways to run practices. Part of your consideration is made for you by the facilities. Gym time is a premium especially in the East, Midwest and any of the rainy states. Generally, no matter where you are practicing, start your practice with stretching drills. Stretching can take many forms. American style tends to by static where International style tends to be a series of slow movements progressing to faster movements. You can research stretching methods and make an age appropriate decision.

When you get gym time and after you stretch, begin every practice with shooting drills. Most games are played in gym settings and players need to gain 'indoor' shooting confidence. After shooting, practice your full court game. I usually begin with transition drills. If you have more time, scrimmage half-court with your best players on defense. Usually, I will run a defense to offense transition. I try to teach the players the rhythm of the game. That is to say when to take the ball to the basket and when to set up our half-court offense.

Your game philosophy is an extension of your personality. Young coaches tend to show their desperation to win. They do not have confidence in their game preparation. Yelling or blaming the officials is titanic move to avoid. Talk about how the game was refereed with your fellow coaches. Leave the players and parents out of this discussion as much as possible. Coaches need to project confidence. Yelling does not reinforce others confidence in you!

Choosing specific Xs and Os can be confusing. Continuity is your friend. A two guard verses a one guard offense may influence how quick your team plays. Zone verses man defense may lean towards shorter or taller teams. Think in terms of your style of play. Then picture the skills your players will need to effectively run your offenses and defenses. Now you are ready to modify existing Xs and Os to create your own plays.

"Keep it simple, when you get too complex you forget the obvious." – Al McGuire

Chapter 7 Creating

By now you have decided to play a fast or slowdown game. You have chosen a few offensive plays and defensive schemes; you are ready to begin creating your own style. Did you know you can have a style of play? Most coaches have a style they copy or mimic from another coach. You can create your own style with a little imagination. I'll give you an idea how I created my style, 'Billy Ball'.

My high school assistants at Rancho Verde nick-named my unique style 'Billy Ball'. It developed over the previous years from my creating plays and schemes from other coaches' offensives and defenses. 'Billy Ball' is a combination gambling, pressure defense and a high octane offense. Early in my career I realized that it is easier to slow down a team offensively than to speed it up. In addition, some game situations require a team to use the game clock to their advantage.

To create within your style you need to understand the offensive or defensive play and have some experience running the plays. If you are new to coaching basketball or any sport, you may be able to lean on a mentor coach and ask what their experiences have been with this or that play. Watching college basketball can be entertaining and educational. Hint: watch ALL 10 players in the game at the same time. Many of us only watch the ball. By watching all 10 players you can get into the game flow and anticipate what may or should have happened. Training your eyes to watch all the players is the best way to watch and evaluate your practices, games and game video.

One caution about creating your special style of ball by modifying these plays should be passed on to you. Sometimes expectations can be a major downer, especially expectations for your players to be able to execute your plays properly. You must instruct your players in the fundamentals needed to execute your plays. You cannot build a house unless you have the proper tools. The same goes for players and play execution. If your players can't pass accurately, they won't be able to run ANY offense properly.

There are lots of books explaining basketball fundamentals. Offensive plays require players to have mastered passing, cutting, screening, setting picks and using picks. These basic skills are the minimum talents needed to run plays properly. Defensively, learning the proper stance, help and recovery principles, box-out and communication skills are your minimum requirements. Your players must understand these before you can expect them to execute your plays.

A famous scholar once said and wrote that there is 'nothing new under the sun'. Most basketball ideas illustrated in books or videos are obviously recycled. But I have rearranged them to make sense in my coaching style.

When you create or modify offensive plays to your own particular style, you must keep in mind the five time-tested offensive moves. They are the pick and roll, the pass and pick away, the give and go, backdoor and the curl moves. Most plays incorporate one or more of these moves.

I begin with teaching the five time-tested offensive moves in an offensive formation. You pick the formation and teach them the options off the five time-tested offensive moves. I call my formation 'Freedom' because it allows our modern players to use any of the moves anytime. It is their choice. I may suggest a specific move based on what defect I see the opponent's defense. Bottom line, players like having the freedom to choose.

One season I had five (5) exceptional starting players. They challenged my offensive creativity. Since they could play any position, I decided to make them all point guards for their own series of plays. The plan evolved so that each player was responsible for teaching his own offense series. Of course each player and I discussed and decided on their particular series. We decided as a team that whoever had the ball when we called for a set offense, that player would call his offensive series. Immediately, five leaders emerged and took control of our set offenses. That was an exceptional team with a fantastic winning record. We had FIVE time tested offenses for most anything opponents threw at us!

Since basketball is a game of habits, your coaching success follows your ability to create ways to teach these habits. After you teach the basic fundamentals in preseason, they must be reinforced during every practice. I created a way to do this by insisting players use one or more fundamentals in each drill or scrimmage.

Generally, I created a warm-up series for most every practice. We run our half-court offenses (without defenses) with whatever options or shots I call out. Then we move to full court with our offensive transition 'cycle'. I run a numbered break for the same habit forming reasons. Through repetition, we build offensive movement habits.

Shooting probably is the bonus of creating offensive play habits. Shooting, especially, the three-pointer is about muscle memory. That's why great shooters practice one shot from one area of the court over and over again. We have creatively called these shots, spot-shots. All the offenses I have created or modified have predictable, open spot-shots. In practices I support my spot-shot theory and have created rebounding schemes and ideas for each shot.

I insist our players take spot-shots during the game. The 'green light' incentivizes players to practice those shots. If your coaching situation has the 'shooting gun', I highly recommend it for some practice situations and for individual workouts.

My rebound theory is that there are no missed shots. We rationalize to our players that they know when we shoot. They should be getting into rebounding positions BEFORE the shot. I created a musical chairs scenario to emphasize anticipating these shots.

Most coaches emphasize offense. But this time tested saying is true. 'Offense wins games but defense wins championships'. That is never truer than when your team is up 2 points with 19 seconds left on the game clock. You can't foul and you have to guard the three-point line!

Your defensive style can be as simple as a sagging man to man or zone. This 'packed it in' style challenges teams to shoot from the outside. Or as adeptly visualized in the movie 'Hoosiers', make them shoot from the cheap seats! Lower level and less skilled teams are easily beaten with this defensive strategy. Of course your team must score, too. So be ready for your opponent to use this style. You must develop a play series and shooters that will destroy these sagging defenses.

My up tempo, rebellious personality leans towards a disrupting defensive style. I have copied and modified ways of disrupting opponents based on the opponents playing style. I use the word WAYS because you will face multiple offensive situations sometimes in a single game but for sure in an entire season. You need to have your team prepared for whatever your opponents utilize.

The disruptive defensive philosophy does not let opponents run offenses like they practice. There are different ways of disrupting depending on your playing level. Generally, higher levels more difficult to disrupt. College and advanced high school players have mastered such plays as the back-door and one on one driving to the basket. When you face a team with very good players your team's defensive intensity becomes a major factor in your team's ability to disrupt.

You must know your player's capabilities and how much they can absorb, remember and still play loose. Basketball cannot be played with uptight players. The game moves too fast. Unlike other popular team sports like baseball and football where there are breaks in the action, basketball is a continuously played sport.

Creating a style you are confident teaching translates into confident players. Create a scoring system your players can execute. Create a defensive system your players understand and want to play. Develop winning HABITS through organized practice sessions. Together your style and your players will be capable of doing and accomplishing extraordinary things.

Teaching habits takes time and patience. It can be boring depending on your ability to create drills and game situations that reinforce the habits that fit your game plan. Basic habits like shooting and rebounding must be balanced with your ideas of how the game should be played.

Create ways that teach HOW to play basketball not just basketball plays!

"Remember that basketball is a game of habits. If you make the other guy deviate from his habits, you've got him." – Bill Russell

Chapter 8 Culture

Whether you like it or not, you are influencing the next generation of kids by coaching them. Ask most adults who played high school or college sports to name a few of their coaches, and they will. Ask these same former players who their 6th grade teacher was and you will probably draw blank stares. Enough said!

Creating a culture for your team is where you become a coach with regrets or a coach with wonderful memories. You can become a smiling, hopeful coach or a negative, sour-puss coach. Your approach will reflex on your actions. As Ralph Waldo Emerson said, "What you do speaks so loudly that I cannot hear what you say."

As a young coach, I definitely was ego driven to the point of coaching with mood swings. I was happy winning. I was 'Oscar the Grouch' when we lost. But a funny thing happened along the way. I became a single parent. That story is for another book!

As a single parent I began to read parenting books. My wife and I separated and we split the kids. I hoped she'd change her mind if we had to share our children. That was a dumb decision on my part. I missed too much of my older daughter's teenage years.

My younger daughter was two (2) years old when we began our coaching journey. I say 'we and our' because this past Christmas I gave her back a musical 'Annie' toy she had when she was four. I had been storing it for some 35 years. I had a local trophy shop glue a bronze plate on it with the inscription "My Best Assistant Coach Ever". She was and now she's a 40 year old parent herself!

The point being I began reading parenting books and applying some of the principles to coaching. The book that influenced me the most was "Your Child's Self-Esteem" by Dorothy Briggs. Her book explains how to create a caring environment for your children. I applied her seven principles to parenting and coaching. My ego driven motivation shifted to that of mostly encouragement.

Dorothy Briggs elaborates on the following seven principles.

- Genuine Encounter
- Trust
- Nonjudgmental
- Cherished
- Owning Feelings
- Empathy
- Unique Growing

With understanding and by using her seven principles, my coaching style gravitated to encouraging players. This change began to pay dividends. Besides feeling more connected with my players, we began winning more games. The rewards of encouraging players continue through today. More than a dozen of my former players are coaching today. I am still in contact with many players that continue to be successful on and off the basketball court. You can have that same satisfaction.

I strongly suggest you get a copy of "Your Child's Self-Esteem" by Dorothy Briggs. Read it. Absorb it. Try using one principle at a time. Soon you will be having, what Ms. Briggs calls a genuine encounter with each of your players.

Creating a positive team culture begins and ends with caring. This phrase says it all. 'Players don't care what you know. They want to know you care!'

We coaches can directly show players how to act towards their teammates and adults. This translates to players sharing the ball on offense. Sharing the ball is old style basketball that works in today's game. Pick up a teammate when they fall to the floor. Point to the teammate that gives you the assist pass. These are only some things that illustrate to all watching that your players care about each other.

I should give you one side bar about the officials. They are not perfect. Part of showing players how to act is showing respect for authority. In basketball that translates into not yelling or demeaning the officials. I firmly believe that yelling coaches at any level don't have confidence in their teaching techniques. Believe it or not, your team will play teams that are better than yours. So be it. Learn and move on without demeaning the officials.

Finally, treat all players similar, but not necessarily the same. You can raise your voice with some players and they will respond positively. Other players may react negatively. Watch you tone and voice volume. That is what it takes to coach most basketball players in today's feelings orientated society!

Personally, I do not run a star system. Some coaches treat their 'star' differently from the rest of the players. I do not base our entire offense or defense on one player's ability. I reason, if the star player gets injured, the team has to make some major adjustments. My system calls for all the players to have guard and forward skills. They should be able to play all our positions. My ideal scoring team has 4 to 7 players in double figures every game. If we are hit with an injury, any adjustments we make are minor.

Keep your eyes on the game. Do not let players' personalities influence your coaching decisions. Ask your self 'What contributions can the player make to the game plan and the team.' Do not qualify his playing time based on any superficial appearances or behavior idiosyncrasy.

Let your behavior be the evidence of a special team culture. Today's buzz-word is 'Family'. You are blending a special type of family. You are combining personalities and basketball with competition. That takes a special person. A coaches' life is about the day you and your players mutually come to respect each other.

"A coach is someone who can give correction without causing resentment." – John Wooden

Chapter 9 Year Around Plan

Some coaches are privileged to have year around programs. High school and college coaches manage players and their improvement most of 12 months a year. The amazing satisfaction coaches' get watching players mature and sharpen their basketball skills is indescribable. Below is my advice to high school head coaches. Although, AAU and middle school coaches may find some parts helpful.

Not all coaches have the luxury of working with their players year around. There are the programs that have only 'in season' players. These players may be multi-sport athletes. Coaches need to analyze their situation and adapt their training program accordingly. No matter your situation, you need to think year-around.

Generally, you can break up your year around plan into four parts according to the calendar seasons. Each part connects with and builds on the next. Beginning in the spring, we work on individual development and improvement. The summer is for practice games and scrimmages. The fall is your preseason. Winter is game time. Within each season fundamentals and conditioning must be your common threads. Each season prepares your team to play at a higher level when your regular season begins.

Most coaches after the post season playoffs get some much needed breathing room from the players and a mental rest from the game. But then the competitive nature of hopeful coaching kicks in and we are off to the races again planning, evaluating and imagining certain players playing specific positions.

The spring season begins with your post-season player evaluations. These evaluations are given to the returning players within a week after the last game. They grade player skills. All returning players are expected to improve their game by working on their weaknesses. With today's technology coaches can keep players involved with emails and texts referring them to specific, skill-development drills posted on the Internet. In addition to drills, I remind players about Colleges' Championship week and the following March Madness games. Players can educate themselves by watching and listening to a month's worth of fantastic college playoff basketball.

Most modern players seek IMMEDIATE success. Consequently, they will continue to go to their strengths when playing competitively. Your job is to convince them to try new moves and develop new skills. Young players need to be made to understand that one good offensive or defensive move does not make a complete player. Scorers that rely on one or two basic moves will be scouted at the higher levels and easily shut down. The coach's job is to insist that they develop multiple options off their signature moves.

A great example is the stand-still 3-point shooter. Closely guarding will eliminate this player's scoring threat. Initially, to encourage the players shooting strength, coaches can show this player how to use jab-steps or swing-pass fakes to create space for their shot. Ideally, a coach should then make this player practice shot fakes to freeze the defense and then to drive to the basket or take one-dribble spot shots.

Coaches use these spring sessions with any number of returning players as their facilities and coaching staff can handle. If a talented player, who didn't play the previous season, wants to join the team, this is a great time to assess their talent, attitude and team value.

Summer sessions are for teaching or reinforcing players in your system. While they are learning you will have scrimmages. During these scrimmages and subsequent summer games coaches encourage players to experiment with the new moves and skills they are trying to master. This is the time to try that new floater shot or to try stealing passes from the helpside position. (I have renamed the helpside/weakside defensive position to my steal-side position. That's an example of creating something unique within your coaching style.)

Some state associations do not allow coaches to instruct players during the off-season. A way to bend that rule is to teach your team's older players the how's and why's of specific drills that directly relate to your game plan and general style of play. Then during open gym sessions you could chat with older players and tell them which drills to use as warm-ups. They run the drills!

Rather than having open 'king of the court' gym sessions in the summer, I prefer skill development and experimentation. Coaches can open the gym for individual shooting sessions. Players can reinforce their ball handling and practice their 3-point shots with the 'shooting gun' or a partner. Hopefully, you or one of your assistants has the free time to spend with individual players.

During the summer, teams play games. I like weekday workout sessions. I have my team attend weekend team camps and tournaments providing we have the funding. During these games you can implement your game plan with you new players. You can experiment with player positions, offensive plays and defenses. After introducing your game plan, ask the players individually, what position they see themselves being successful.

Evaluating different players at different positions often surprises a coach. The summer is the best time to do that. I am continually surprised by the shorter players wanting to play post positions and taller players that want to play guard. Within my style of play, they both get their chances.

Most coaches use the fall for teaching and reinforcing fundamentals within the team concept. If you have stressed fundamentals during the spring and summer, your fall workouts will be more productive. Now your team can practice your game plan at a slower developmental pace with you pointing out where and how to use the appropriate fundamental to the player's advantage. My classic line comes from the heart. I tell players I want them to look good in front of the crowds. Do not embarrass yourselves. "**LOOK LIKE A BASKETBALL PLAYER!**" I usually follow up with "then you will play like a player".

During the winter, coaches come alive. Playing games is the ultimate test for your philosophy and your system it illustrates. Game specifics will be discussed in a later chapter. My advice to coaches is to NEVER engrave your philosophy and system in stone. Always be open to modifications depending on your coaching circumstances.

Weight lifting rounds off your player's year-around conditioning. During the off-season, have your players lift for strength. That is to lift heavy and increase your player's maximums for their major muscle groups. Many weight lifting programs achieve this goal. Your coaching situation will dictate which weight lifting program you advise your players to use.

I did my master's thesis on 'in-season weight lifting.' My theory was that lifting light weights for a high number of repetitions would maintain established pre-season maximums. My results proved that theory. Not only did we maintain maximums, but some players actually increased their maximums. Their increased maximums weren't staggering but they were measurable. Ideally, if you're doing in-seasoning weight lifting, do it BEFORE practice. We had sandwiches and drinks during the rest time (study hall) between lifting and practices. Having that much team time after school united our players and coaches like very few other activities I had previously tried.

As an experienced coach, I can only smile at some of the conditions I have had to coach basketball. One of my favorites was coaching a college all-star team for Athletes in Action. We played on a rural countryside outdoor court, east of Lima, Peru. The outside cement court was cracked and broken apart with weeds growing through the cracks. We played at night with five 40 watt light bulbs strung diagonally across the court. During warm-ups we broke the glass backboard at one end. The host team made us use that basket, now without a backboard, for the entire game. My coaching strategy was only shoot swishes and to trap in the VERY dark corner at the far end of the court. One freethrow we shot bounced backwards off the front of the rim and hit the rod support that was behind where the backboard should have been. And then the ball went in. We cracked up laughing on the bench! Can't help thinking of the cushy conditions we have to coach here in the United States!

"The best teamwork comes from men who are working independently toward one goal in unison." – James Cash Penney

Chapter 10 In Season Practices

John Wooden taught me that 95% of all game situations can be practiced. That is good advice for an experienced coach, but what about new coaches? How do you prepare for the unknown?

My advice is to watch college basketball and listen to the commentators. Most basketball commentators have had playing or coaching experiences. They can give you their wisdom and insights into the game. Listen and learn from their point of view. Then adapt what you like in their thoughts to your style and philosophy.

With or without experience you can create practice plans to reinforce your style and philosophy. The goal is for your team to play your style in practice, then in games. To reach this goal, develop a general practice plan for your season's practices. This plan covers general areas of play under a specific heading. Remember to teach HOW to play basketball not only basketball plays!

Since basketball is a game of habits, your coaching must follow your ability to teach habits. After you teach the basic fundamentals in preseason, they must be reinforced them during every practice. A way to do that is to insist you see one or more of those fundaments in each drill or scrimmage.

Every practice should include time for the following areas: warm-up/stretching, shooting, defense, transition, offense, special plays, freethrows and a cold down exercise. Your style will dictate your sequence and times for each. Two or more of these sections can be combined. For example, you can warm-up by running your half-court offenses in a dummy mode. You may scrimmage emphasizing defense, boxing out and running the transition to offense. Once over half-court have your guards decide whether to go for the score or set up your half-court offense. Scrimmaging in the form of this drill teaches players poise under pressure. UNLV's Jerry Tarkanian won the NCAA Championship in 1989-90 using this practice method for scrimmaging.

Your preseason practice may include more teaching and explaining than your in season practices. So adjust the time allotted for each section of your practice outline accordingly. Below is my general practice outline. At this point in my coaching career, filling this out only takes a few minutes. Young coaches may have to put some time in it. You need to visualize what offenses and defenses you want your team to be capable of running and when in the season you want them to run them.

Shooting – while team players are arriving for practice (shooting form drill back to freethrows – then 15 footers – finally 3 pointers)

Stretching – 5 minutes (I present our thought for the day and what we want to accomplish today)

Warm-up – (time depends on where you are in the season - dummy half-court offenses)

Transition drills – 10 – 15 minutes

Water/Freethrows – 3 minutes (important especially in dry climates)

Defense - (usually half-court fundamental - time depends on where you are in season)

Transition to Offense - (time depends on where you are in season)

Water/Freethrows

Offense vs half-court defense - (time depends on where you are in season)

Special Plays – (end of game ahead, behind, full-court, out of bounds, etc.)

Freethrows – (Line up team on end line under basket. One by one each player comes out to shoot a freethrow. We run lines or do Marine burpees on misses.)

Cool down (usually making 10 freethrows or something like that)

Your practice philosophy will evolve over time. Remember that at the beginning of the preseason you will use more practice time for teaching. In season practices usually reinforce preseason ideas within you offenses, defenses and transitions style. Midseason you are adding some modifications to these for variety to keep the players from getting stale. Nearing the end of the season, practices can be shorter and try to add more fun things as rewards for playing 'hard and together'.

Post-season practices are difficult. If your main players are competitive, they will set the team example. If they are looking ahead to other sports or whatever, coaching becomes a focus problem. We discuss this further in the 'Playoffs' chapter.

A few reminders:

Relax and have fun. Your team goal should be to get better every practice and every game. Learn from you loses and challenge your team further on the wins.

Put 2-4 fundamentals in one full court drill. This saves practice time and adds to the game's continuity.

Talk - 1 minute to 10 of activity.

Maintain a 'poise' theme throughout practice.

Teach what anticipate means, especially on defense.

For every play whether offense, defense, shooting, etc players should have a counter move.

Incorporate want drills during the preseason before choosing your team.

Hold to your standards - Play Hard - Play Together – Have Fun

Experiment with specific drills and plays. You can fill in the blanks with you favorites or learn some new ones from all the basketball literature floating around.

"When opportunity comes, it's too late to prepare" – John Wooden

.

Chapter 11 Conditioning

Conditioning takes care of itself. Coaches that spend separate time periods of practice to condition their athletes waste precious repetition practice time. Remember, basketball is a game of habits. Repeating and forming those habits is your key to player's success.

Most practice situations, except in the professional ranks, exist within specific time limits. High school and college coaches have limits to the amount of practice time they can spend with players. This practice time is precious and should not be wasted on conditioning.

Of the many reasons for this approach, player responsibility tops my opinion. Players that do not work hard in practice executing team and individual drills will not be in shape no matter how much time you spend on conditioning. Their half-hearted efforts that keep them from being in top physical condition with drills and scrimmaging carries over to all conditioning activities.

I favor attacking the conditioning problem with competition, timed drills and active substitution policies. This combination has served my teams to the point that running for the sake of running is a foreign concept to my players.

Competition intrinsically favors players with winning attitudes. Losing is not part of their personality. Take note of the players that win competitive drills. These are the players that win games.

Two on two, three on three, four on four games, rebounding drills, and one on one guarding situations are a few types of competitions we use in practice. We use several types of prizes. Early in the season we may give the winner a choice of push-ups, crunches, Marine burpees or lines. The loser does the leftover choice. For example: we will play 4 on 4 shell. For every defensive stop a team earns a point. The first team to 3 stops wins. Winners choose between 10 push-ups or 15 Marine burpees. The goal is to get players playing at game speed and finish the drill with some minor muscle building activity.

Timing our drills works to teach players the value of the clock and encourages their competitive nature. A great example of our early season timed activity is full court lay-ups. We use 12 players. They must alternately make a lay-up or rebound a shot, then hustle back to the opposite line at half-court and do it all over again at the other end of the court. We give them a minute and count the number of made lay-ups. We have a specific number of makes as a goal. If we don't achieve that number, we all do Marine burpees or something similar. Then we do the drill again.

Beginning or finishing practices with competitive shooting drills encourages players to shoot at game speed with game like pressure. Losers do crunches, winners cheer them on!

Early in the season, we like to play as many players as possible. This motivates players in two meaningful ways. First, everyone gets a chance to show what they can do in game situations. Secondly, I let the players know that not playing hard will earn them a seat on the bench. The worst punishment for most players is sitting on the bench during practice or games. I make players not participating in drills or scrimmages jump rope during practices. During games, I ask them questions like, "What defense or offense is the opponent using." If they can't answer or don't know, they don't play until they know. That's my standard!

During games I evaluate if they're playing hard by watching players sprint the transitions or if they're in defensive helpside stances. If they don't sprint or are not in their stance, they will be substituted for. I try to always encourage them when they come out to rest on the bench. Of course, most will say that they're not tired. My stock answer is "Why aren't you running the transition or in your stealside stance?" If they continue the conversation, I ask them to sit at the end of the bench. And that we'll check the video tomorrow! My players figure out early on that to keep playing in games, they must run the transition and play in their defensive stance. Our players learn quickly what's acceptable and what is not!

The real secret to conditioning is simple. Once your players understand what's expected of them in each of your drills, use the full court to run these drills. I advocate using a few well thought out drills every practice, rather than teaching new drills all the time. Many drills like 3 on 2 continuation features all the basic fundaments players need to be successful. I choose different fundamentals to emphasize everyday. That way the players are familiar with drill's mechanics and there's no lost teaching time. The players perform the fundaments to my satisfaction or we stop the drill for some reminder drilling. Players want to play. They hate reviewing basic fundamentals.

Conditioning is the players' responsibility. Competitive players tend to be exceptionally conditioned athletes. They work and play hard. Therefore they out run, out play and out think lesser conditioned athletes, especially in the heat of battle. My teams might lose games, but it's not from lack of conditioning. I pride myself on coaching players to be responsible, confident athletes.

"I don't count my sit-ups at the beginning; I only start counting when it starts hurting because they're the only ones that count." – Muhammad Ali (aka. Cassius Marcellus Clay Jr.)

Chapter 12 Games

When we think of game management we coaches think of strategy. Planning and strategizing long ahead of game time helps coaches to approach games with confidence. That confidence translates to confident players walking on the court at the start of any game. What happens next makes marines of us all. We improvise, adapt and overcome!

We have already learned from Coach John Wooden that 95% of all game situations can be practiced. My advice for coaches is to include in your style of play all the game situations you can imagine. If you are having trouble imagining more than a few, ask more experienced coaches what they would do to counter your game plan. You could ask a fellow coach to scout your team and read the scouting report. Then you create counters to the weakness found on the scouting report.

For example you are playing a man offense. Your opponent switches from a man defense to a zone. Now your team should have practiced your zone offense and be able to switch into it on the court without calling a time out. And if the opponent switches into a DIFFERENT zone, your players need to adapt again without a time out.

Imagine your team running a man offense and the opponents throw a 2-3 zone at you. You counter with a 1-3-1 zone offense. Then opponents switch to a 1-3-1 or a 1-2-2 zone. You counter with a 2-1-2 zone offense. Practicing these types of situations gives your team confidence to make the necessary changes seamlessly during the games. Coaches learn these strategic moves during your philosophy, exploring, choosing and creating phases of becoming a coach.

Respect is my trigger word for games. Coaches should exemplify success and respect. We have already discussed a quality relationship style with players according to Ms. Dorothy Briggs. That respect style can also be applied to game situations.

Consider what progresses before, during and after a game. Great coaches prepare using the same progression EVERY game. This same progression of pregame events accomplishes a number of reassuring things. Players know exactly what to expect 99% of the time.

The time players need to be at game site before games should be the same for all games. I like my players to get acclimated to their surroundings. If we are playing an away game without a game before us, I generally tell my players I will arrive early with the basketballs. Some choose to arrive early. When they do, I encourage them to take as many warm up shots as they wish before our players warm up as a team.

We go into locker room near the end of the 3rd quarter of the game being played before us. If there is no game, I try to get into the locker room about 40 minutes before game time. I let the players relax and get dress, ready to play.

Our pregame talk is about 10 minutes long. It should grab their attention with a positive observation about our team. One I have used in the past went something like this. "After watching several dozen Division I teams practice, I can honestly say our last two practices this week were as competitive as any I have observed!" Then, I point out our strengths that should give us an edge in this game. I usually do that with some phase of the game we have emphasized during the previous week. My psychology being to remind players we are going to play WHAT we practiced.

Focusing on our team's readiness improves team confidence and gives a boost to all aspects of our teamwork ethic. I will let the players relax for a few minutes to collect themselves while I talk individually to each player about something to focus on when they play.

Some of us have the luxury of scouting opponents. Some coaches scout very little or not at all, John Wooden style. I do not like to talk about the other team with any praise or comments of admiration. I usually make defensive assignments based on the team's style of play. Sometimes I tell each player which closeout to use. Sometimes I will wait until after watching the opponent's warm up. My personality and attitude are on display before games. We are going to destroy whoever we play.

I will use descriptive words meaning that very thing every game.

Sometimes I will extend an invitation to my assistant coaches to contribute to our pre-game talk. Usually they reinforce something I said but from a different angle. When I work as an assistant sometimes the head coach extends the same invitation to me. I point out something positive and encouraging from our previous week of practices or games. I will use this sort of event to build team confidence.

Before one playoff game when I was asked to speak. I mentioned what I observed when our team walked into the opponent's gym earlier that afternoon. The crowd lining our walkway from the bus to the gym was impressed with our muscular size and ethnic diversity. I translated there awe to our high school players with my impression from the crowd's reaction. I said if we put on UCLA uniforms, the crowd would not have even questioned that we WERE UCLA. We played with such confidence that we destroyed this league champion in this playoff game with our junior varsity players playing most of the forth quarter. We continued playing that season deep into the Southern California CIF playoffs.

Pregame warm ups last anywhere from 10 to 20 minutes. We use the same routine every game. Only the length of each section changes with our warm-up time. We have a routine that finishes with lots of outside shooting and freethrows.

Our pre-game, starters talk on the bench is simple and straight forward. I remind them to attack the basket offensively. Defensively, I will challenge the players to see who will get our first steal. Depending on our aggressiveness, I will continue to up the steals number for some practice reward privileges the coming week.

When starting the game I make sure my subs are lined up on the bench where I can talk with them when necessary. Mostly, I just start talking with my assistant coach.

During the game my assistant coach conversation continues. My rule for subbing players in a competitive game is no trotting the transitions and/or standing up on defense. Through my practices I repeat that stealing passes can only happen with anticipation from a ready, defensive stance.

When certain players get into foul trouble, I encourage them to play smart. I don't necessarily pull them from the game. All my players know my foul theory. If subconsciously you do not want to play, you make stupid fouls. Once in a blue moon some official will intentionally go after a player. But that is rare and can be predicted by the coaches or players previous interactions with them.

Coaches should respect the officials. I feel that coaches who constantly argue with the officials DO NOT have confidence in their coaching ability. This sentiment goes for all levels. Arguing sets a bad example for anyone around the team and especially the players.

Officials are human and make mistakes just like coaches. A non-judgmental approach towards the officials pays dividends for future games.

Our half time talks are partly a rest and recovery period. I encourage energy drinks, oranges or Snicker bars for the players to munch on. I will point out what is working for us. Most importantly, I prepare the floor leaders for what adjustment the opponents will make. I mainly talk with each of the players how to boost their contributions to our team effort. I try to do this when I substitute too.

Timeout talks should have ONE general team idea. I try to speak in short descriptive phrases like: run the transaction or look for a steal when they ..... or talk more on defense when they ...... Then if you have time, give specific directions to specific players. Some instructions may sound like: Johnnie – you can drive on the guy guarding you; Jesse use the 'shooter' close out on your man, he's killing us with 3-pointers.

Some timeouts require you give the team a play. Hopefully, you have already practiced it and only have to remind your players how to execute it properly. Rarely have I had to draw up a brand new play for a situation. If you expect to do that regularly, practice drawing up fresh plays during your special play section in practice.

End of game hand shaking is a sign of good sportsmanship. I have had only one memorable hand shaking incident. My team had lost a high level, semi-final Southern Section CIF playoff game. While shaking hands with the opponents, who featured two right-out-of-high-school NBA picks, they tried to recruit my best young player. He eventually went DI to Oregon State. I acted silly and said to the opposing head coach, "Nice game for the best team Nike and money could buy!" The head coach chased me towards our lock room before his assistant turned him around. The next day my Athletic Director said my comment made it into the LA Times sports section. All I could do was smile. That team won CIF AND the California State Championship that year.

Our post game talks consist of what is next. Sometimes, I will give high fives to some for their exceptional plays. I especially try to complement players that need pumping up! I have learned not to make major game evaluations UNTIL after watching the game video. After the games my feeling sometimes interferes with what should be a logical, factual based game assessment.

Our post game evaluation happens while I watch game video, do the stats and make notes for our next practice. I have found that I take the most accurate team stats. Videos don't lie! At our next practice I will emphasize our game faults and praise the good things we did. I will usually refer to both during our regular practice drills.

Some final thoughts include:

Remind your players to play with poise especially on the offense. John Wooden said, "Be quick, but don't hurry."

The more game adjustments you make and have practiced, the more you keep your opponents off balance.

To all players coming off the bench whether subs or resting starters - come off bench READY to get into flow of game AND CONTRIBUTE. Stay warm or warmed up mentally!

Basketball is a game of 'scoring runs'. In basketball terms that translates into scoring lots of points with opponents scoring only a few if any. Coaches need to realize this fact and stay level headed during those runs, whichever way the score is moving. The usual strategy is to call time outs when the opponents are in their scoring run.

Plan what you'll do for as many game situations as possible. When you have successfully taught how to make game adjustments and adaptability to your players, game management is fun!

"On good teams coaches hold players accountable, on great teams players hold players accountable" – Joe Dumars

Chapter 13 Playoffs

End of the season playoffs are like a coaches' final exam. They measure a coaches' teaching effectiveness. No matter the playing level, playoffs separate you team from the rest of the pack. ANYTHING can happen during the playoff season!

Your team should be excited for playoff games. Still, post-season high school practices have a problem unique to specific players. If your main players are competitive, they will set the tone. However, if some players are looking ahead to other sports or post season activities, coaching the team may become a focus problem for these players. A few tweaks in your practices will help maintain their focus.

A few practice modifications are obvious. The first of which is reinforcing the basic fundamentals that got your team in the playoffs. Some early pre-season practice themes and drills should be reinforced and re-emphasized.

Next is to shorten practices by 15 to 45 minutes. If your players aren't in shape now, they won't be before the first playoff game. Leave extra gym time for your dedicated shooters. Some shooters will sleep in the gym if you let them. I have found that players volunteering for extra shooting practice will play more confidently and usually want to take the game deciding shot, if there is one!

Play competitive shooting games. Keep heavy contact drills to a minimum. Run you half-court offense within realistic game situations. We do that during regular season practices. You may want to add the use the gym's scoreboard and the PA system with crowd noise to simulate game pressure. For example, it's the end of the game, you're down one point, 11 seconds in the game and you must score to win. Do the same with out-of-bounds plays. Practice those time sensitive, especially end of game, scenarios from losing and winning perspectives.

Freethrows will decide close games. This truth is magnified 100 fold in playoff games. We began and end our practices with freethrows throughout the entire season. We cultivate the 'I want to be on the freethrow line' attitude especially at the end of a game. Defense wins championships with freethrows sealing the victory!

Playoffs should be a celebration for the players. They should be excited by the challenge of the one and done survival scenario. Unfortunately, many coaches move toward playoffs too seriously. As with a coaches' approach to the officials, playoffs tell a tale of a coaches' confidence in his teaching abilities as much as it is a talent contest.

When you begin coaching, aim for the playoffs but don't be discouraged. Post-season winning eludes many coaches. Usually, experienced players, on experienced teams win during the post-season. For younger teams, I incorporate the idea of getting better every practice and every game. So, when the post-season comes, we are just about as good as humanly possible and ready for playoff games!

At the high school level, my philosophy leans towards giving younger players game experience. I always try to cultivate younger players on my varsity teams. My most prolific post-season run came two years after I started four sophomores on the varsity. We lost our share of games against teams with experienced upper class players that year.

With those sophomores starting, our varsity team was 7 and 18 that year. The school's administrators questioned my coaching skills. Luckily my athletic director had my back. The next year we were 19 and 6. Those players' senior year we were 30 and 4 at the end of our playoff run. We had won two big county preseason tournaments, a second place finish another tourney. We lost to the eventually CIF and State champion. Needless to say, those same questioning administrators congratulated me on a great coaching job that season. Little did they know that this team's greatness began two years earlier.

With patience and a few years of coaching wisdom you will realize that your team can get playoff wins against teams physically better and more talented than your team. We did with average kids. Our team culture was exceptional. Each player had their own personality strengths and weaknesses. Their backgrounds were varied.

Our school and gym were nothing special. What was special were the player's hearts, determination and team bond.

Those three years, the players felt our coaching staff's bond and they imitated it on the court. After three years of being together I didn't have to do much game coaching. I pretty much chatted with my assistants looking for GLMs. Once in a while I would walk the sidelines to keep the subs in line or to get some exercise.

When that particular playoff run began, all I had to do was look in our player's eyes to see what was happening. They were so well coached that they would call their own timeouts and knew what adjustments we needed to make. That team grew during those three years into a post-season force. We were beating league champions at their gym by 25 or more points. Six games into the playoffs we hit a 'brick wall'. The team we played had two players drafted by the NBA after their senior year. They slammed the door on our postseason run.

The point of the above story is that your teams can beat better, more physical teams. For us it took taking our lumps for a season of playing with young players. Our tallest player was 6'3". The other four starters were 5'6" to 6'. We weren't big. We were strong where it counted, in our player's hearts!

My assistant coaches for that team were exceptional. I advise young coaches to become head coaches as soon as an opportunity arises. When you do look for assistants, find ones that will learn and coach your system. Sometimes individuals new to coaching are your best choice. Older coaches tend to bring their own style. If it's different than yours or doesn't compliment yours, that could be disruptive and confusing to the players.

You will need quality assistants. Don't be afraid to delegate practice, game and/or management responsibilities to them. However, remember to follow up on what they do. They are an extension of you.

I find it difficult to give you advice on how to be a good assistant. My personality tends towards being the leader of a team, not part of the leadership. My years spent as an assistant were beneficial, but not from an Xs and Os point of view. I learned how coaches relate to players. My best advice to assistant coaches is to be loyal and ask clarifying questions to learn the head coaches' game plan and his philosophy about the game.

Playoff games are primarily about controlling the game's tempo, turnovers and making shots. Scouting helps prepare your defense and gives you some direction as to which offenses in your game plan you need to practice.

Because of the win or done aspects of playoff games, teams tend to panic earlier in a game as soon as they think they may lose. Teach your players game poise. Explain to them that games are like running a marathon. Runners pace themselves for a strong finish. They don't panic if they fall behind for a bit of the race.

I always keep a few surprises within our game plan and don't use them regularly during the season. I'll pull them out during the playoffs as we need a boost or to change the game's pace.

Your style, when fully developed, should control the tempo of all your games. Playing your tempo during playoff games, keeps your players comfortable and confident. Usually teams that control the games tempo win playoff games.

If other teams dictate your game's tempo, you may want to make slight modifications in your defensive style. In my game plan we disrupt the other team's offense. We force tough shots. Then we focus on boxing-out, rebounding, running and scoring quickly. Our goal is to outscore opponents by a lot of points.

Complimenting our defense, I stress controlling the offensive boards. In addition to running to score, we run to rebound in our half court offense. We 'run' to rebound by emphasizing predictable, practiced spots shots.

During the season, coaches get obsessed with turnovers. Playoff games are often won or lost because of turnovers. I believe lack of concentration causes unforced turnovers. Hustle turnovers sometimes can't be helped. Coaches need to know the difference and respond accordingly.

Loss of focus can be a distraction or fatigue problem during playoffs. Early in your season you need to demand total focus when players are on the court. Distractions like grades, parents, friends, car problems or whatever needs to be handled before or after practices or games. If they can't be, then coaches must instruct players to leave practice, and take care of their business. Then come back to the team. Fatigue problems reflect on a coach's practice policies. By using full court, continuous type of competitive drills and scrimmages, coaches will condition players for a full, 32 minute game. Coaches can also affect a player's efficiency with game situation, strategic substitutions.

At the beginning of your season your team sets obtainable goals. At playoff time evaluate how well the team has accomplished them. Bragging to your players about how well the team has achieved and surpassed these goals builds a player's confidence. Ultimately, this transfers to confident team play. Only confident players resist losing their poise in tight game situations especially during playoffs. Bottom line, your team is better than they think. Go back to those earlier season goals and give your team positive, well-earned feedback.

During the year-around program, coaches will have had the opportunity to review most every situation present in basketball. During the playoffs, you can look back at the season and think about adjustments you could have made. Then you can incorporate them into next year's program.

By anticipating situations that may or may not happen to your team, you can expand on how you expect players to react/respond to whatever happens. I say react/respond because there is a difference. Coaches should teach that reactions happen instantaneously like habits occur from muscle memory and repetition. Responses occur when the person's action to a stimulus gets evaluated in their brain before their muscle-action kicks in.

My 'ICE' example has come in handy many times throughout my coaching career. My style of fast paced basketball has a tendency to beat teams by wide margins. When that happens on an opponent's home court or in tournament championship games, opponent players may get angry and try to provoke a fight between teams. Several of my better teams listened to my caution about angry opposing players. When my teams play well, even the subs are effective. I do not change playing styles and the points continue to add up!

The way I impress this reaction/response difference is with a real world example. I hypnotize a person being in a bar drinking a beer with a sports game on TV. The guy next to you wants to pick a fight by insulting your mamma or whatever. Your choice is to fight or walk away. If you walk away, the situation gets defused. If you fight, win or lose, the guy leaves and comes back into the bar with a gun. Bang you're dead! Unfortunately, many of my players can relate to that happening in their neighborhoods! Lesson hopefully learned.

When I notice opponents beginning to play rough and take cheap shots at my players, I call out 'ICE'. In our team's language it means stay cool, we coaches see what's happening and are telling the officials to keep watch. Do not get baited into fighting or even talking smack. During the season my ICE 'respond verses react' talk is one of the things we discuss during our pre-season stretching sessions.

High hopes and dreams accompany playoff games. Whatever side of the game we finish, ICE is still the concept the entire team can relate. With today's game being full of 'smack talk', 'ICE' has kept many questionable player situations from blowing up.

There is no easy way to end a season filled with expectations, relationships and tons of fun. Playoffs provide a clean break because only winners move on. I generally approach every playoff game with an attitude that we ARE winners, maybe just not this game. There are only a few teams that finish the season winning their last game. Generally, I'll tell the team, this wasn't our year. Next year starts later this spring!

Coach Pat Riley, five NBA championships, had a philosophy for every occasion. During the regular season "You rotate eight players". As your team goes through the playoffs his rotation began to shrink. Riley said how his teams go through playoff games with his top players. "You play seven, you use six and you trust five."

"In the playoffs, will beats skill." - Kevin Constantine

Chapter 14 Press

Getting press coverage for you team, program or school can be like a two-edged sword. Publicity can attract fans to your games. It can also be a forum for discontented players or parents. For example, some parents think their son or daughter is destined to become a professional player and they don't like how you assign playing time.

Earlier I mentioned that most coaches get hired by teams with losing records in the immediate past. Crowds at their games are usually small. You come in and turn a program around and start winning. Winning brings in the people and press coverage.

The first media words out of your month should be thanking the administration for giving you a chance to coach these marvelous players. The next words should complimentary towards the parents and the community support. Finally, exhort the players and their contributions. Let people know that your team has a 'family' atmosphere.

If the press asks you to tell them a little about yourself, give them resume information. Keep it general without discussing personal things. NEVER talk politics. NEVER stereotype people or situations. Answer open ended questions with open ended answers. If Barbara Walters ever shows up, then and only then can you get down to particulars about yourself.

Today's social media has expanded avenues for disgruntled people to post their feelings. Basketball fans may use a variety of general media outlets to vent. The most popular media outlets are sports blogs, Twitter, Facebook, etc. Wherever is handy they'll use to post critical comments about coaches and players alike. As a coach, you MUST advise players to ignore the negativity and not to participate in any discussions.

I recall one high school situation where one of my players was the second leading scorer in the county. He had a propensity for not playing defense. He would get two or three quick, stupid fouls in a game. Then his previous coaches would tell him to back off defensively so he wouldn't get more fouls. So he played lazy defense and wanted to take all the shots on offense. The other players let him.

I did the opposite. I told him I would bench him after two fouls to keep him out of foul trouble for later in the game. He sat on the bench dismayed. His parents attacked me for benching him. They went so far as to hold impromptu meetings in the school's parking lot to get me fired.

The player, to his credit did start playing realistic defense, but his parents still didn't like my substitution rotation. They felt their child was destined for the NBA and should be on the floor the entire game. They attacked me through every social media avenue you could imagine. I became famous among coaching circles far from my school. Amazingly, he still maintained his scoring average with less playing time!

The situation resolved itself when his parents transferred him to a neighboring high school. That coach asked me later the next season to take him back! The parents were his worst nightmare!

As a coach of children and teenagers, you MUST remember that all your coaching and off court actions are subject to public review. If parents or fans are out to get you fired, they will try to blow minor situations into major issues. Act as if your loving grandmother and mother were watching your public life. Privately, go to the hills of Afghanistan if you want to do anything controversial.

As a rule of thumb say nothing negative about anyone. Whether you have a microphone or not in your face, try to compliment people, especially other coaches. I've learn that locker room talk among coaches can get back to district administrators. Some principals take offense when they hear a coach say that they have no 'balls' for discipline. Coaches get fired over locker room talk they thought were private conversations.

Build up all players. Use language your grandmother would approve. To me, cursing indicates a lack of or limited vocabulary. Try to use traditional words to explain or express your delight or displeasure.

As a college coach I had our players take speech or communications classes. I would also have some fun with them by having mock press interviews. I wanted them to be able to express themselves as the bright, young gentlemen they were. Most of the time, they did!

You want your players to represent well. When we elaborate about representing we begin with represent themselves as intelligent, caring individuals. Then we remind players that they are representing their family, school, team and community. That burden is highlighted when our 'have fun' standard is applied.

When you get that high school or college coaching position, get to know the local press people. You don't have to be their best buds, but you should know their names and what publications they represent. When you have team events like fundraisers, camps or whatever, you can pass on the information to the public through your press acquaintances and their publications.

Some coaches use Instagram, Twitter, Facebook, etc to feature players and their programs. Again I encourage you to procedure with caution. Social media can be exploitive. Do not release specific information about players or coaches. MaxPreps and other school athletic reporting sites have filters in place to make reporting about your team safer. As a coach remember to act as if you and your players live in glass houses!

"A person really doesn't become whole, until he becomes a part of something that's bigger than himself." – Jim Valvano

Let the Peacocks Fly

Coaching Basketball: Unboxed Wisdom
flowed as if a river of thoughts from my
experiences. The book's goal is to encourage
basketball coaches to create their own
philosophy and style of play. The rewards of
doing so multiply the longer you coach.

The mature, evolved coach possesses a
GROWTH Mindset. This is a mindset that fosters
and embarrasses learning and the efforts to learn
more. A Growth Mindset leads to progress and
greater achievement. While this book doesn't
cover every possible topic in the vast subject of
coaching basketball, it does span the author's
coaching experiences. Observing basketball from
the inside as a coach and outside knowing the
game's idiosyncrasies has given me insights
beyond the average coach. Without a Growth
Mindset, my experiences would have been in
vain.

Dr. Carol Dweck developed her Growth
Mindset after observing thousands of students.
She asked the question 'Why do some students
rebound from failure and others don't?' Those
that rebound from failure spend more time
becoming high achievers. I encourage you to
Google 'Growth Mindset'. Research Dr. Dweck's
ideas. In a similar way to incorporating Dr. Briggs
ideas into your coaching philosophy, Dr. Dweck's
ideas fit comfortably into the picture of a mature
coach.

Coaches with a Growth Mindset seek players with the same attitude. Athletics is about achievement. Coaches that try to be better coaches constantly push players to achieve more. Improvement is the mark of coaching and playing excellence.

Basketball is an enjoyable game to watch. Watching my teams improve and have fun on the court is an awesome feeling. As players become more self-directed, playing the game as I taught them, the more I can sit back and enjoy the fruits of my labor. That's why I try to literally sit on the bench during games. My rational resides in the confidence that I have created a team culture and integrated it with my game plan/philosophy.

I am a fan of the college game. I enjoy the youthful enthusiasm and teamwork aspects of college players. When I coach high school, I try to elevate my players' skill level close to that of college players. True, that is not a realistic goal for all teams and players. But the efforts to become as good as humanly possible at any level is an admirable goal.

During our third or fourth game this past season I was sitting on the bench talking with one of my players. We were beating up on some team because my junior varsity players were playing like college players. The player asked why my expectations were so high for our team. He said, "After all we were only sophomores and freshmen." We talked back and forth on the bench while the second team was on the court.

He concluded with, "Coach, let the peacocks fly!" He was saying, 'We got it coach!'

I thought about his comments that weekend. I realized I was treating my players like college age players. I took his comment to heart, but didn't lower my expectations. I tweaked my approach to hide my real expectations. I smiled more and lightened up during practices and games still maintaining the established standards.

Amazing what happened. The players became more self-directed. In truth, I HAD taught them enough about the game of basketball already. They actually learned and applied practice and previous game lessons. They didn't need me to win games. All they needed me for was to reinforce our game plan by calling some of our early transition plays. They knew the defense. They knew what offensive adjustments to make depending on the opponent's set defense. My contributions became directing our practices and enjoying our games.

If you enjoy watching your creation play, 'Let the Peacocks Fly!'

If you have that kind of confidence in teaching your game plan - 'Let the Peacocks Fly!'

I will never forget what this old coach learned from that wise player, 'Let the Peacocks Fly!'

"Never give up. Failure and rejection are just the first steps to succeeding." – Jim Valvano

73908512R00064

Made in the USA
Columbia, SC
08 September 2019